Peter Schreiner:

EFFECTIVE USE OF THE
AGILITY LADDER FOR SOCCER

Library of Congress
Cataloging - in - Publication Data

Effective Use of the Agility Ladder for
Soccer
Schreiner, Peter

ISBN No. 1-59164-060-1
Lib. of Congress Catalog No. 2003107978
© 2003

Photos by
Institute for Youth Soccer
www.ifj96.de

Diagrams by
Dr. Marion Becker-Richter

Printed by
DATA REPRODUCTIONS
Auburn, Michigan

Reedswain Publishing
612 Pughtown Road
Spring City, PA 19475
800.331.5191
www.reedswain.com
info@reedswain.com

Contents:

Introduction

The agility ladder - a practical conditioning aid

The agility ladder is an important aid for conditioning speed, agility and coordination. It is simple to transport and set up. Ever more coach-

es and instructors are discovering the benefits of the agility ladder in their training sessions. This book should help you get to know the wide variety of possible drills and tasks and thus to use the agility ladder effectively. Numerous models of the agility ladder are available at a range of prices. The professional version shown in the illustrations in this book (see below) is relatively heavy, can be split into two halves, which can be arranged in an L-shape, and has a device for easy transportation. The rungs of the ladder can be adjusted.

Using the agility ladder effectively

✓ Three drill levels have proven their usefulness with the agility ladder (see p 5).

✓ The coach should take account of the age and ability levels of the players.

✓ Allow plenty of pauses - the players should only practice when they are relaxed.

✓ Use the agility ladder regularly (the players' speed, agility and coordination will improve rapidly.)

Three drill levels:

The coach must introduce new and unfamiliar movements gradually, so that the players can progress step by step. Speed and fast footwork should only be encouraged when the players can carry out the movements correctly.

1. Familiarization
In the first phase, the players try out the new movement. They must concentrate on carrying out the movement perfectly. The coach should correct any errors immediately. The drills often seem to be very easy, so the players may underestimate them and try to perform them too quickly. Speed and fast footwork follow automatically as the players gain in confidence.

2. Increasing the tempo
In the second phase, the players perform the movements more quickly. The focus is still on executing the movements properly. From the very beginning, the coach must ensure that the players remain at least four fields apart (field = space between two rungs of the agility ladder).

3. Maximum speed
In the third phase the players should be able to perform the movements properly at top speed. The arm movement is very important.

The agility ladder promotes:
✓ Speed and fast reactions
✓ Concentration
✓ Balance
✓ Coordination.

Suitable surface for the agility ladder

The surface on which the ladder is rolled out is very important. Grass, artificial grass and clay surfaces are the most suitable, because the agility ladder adheres best to them. Indoors, agility ladders - especially if they are light - have to be secured with adhesive tape. If this is not enough, small boxes can be placed on the two ends of the ladder and incorporated into the drills (final jump over or onto a box).

When training sessions are held on a grass pitch, the coach should seek a suitable spot, as the use of the agility ladder can cause considerable wear on the grass. Areas on the edge or alongside the pitch are best.

Coordination - a prerequisite for top performance

Well-developed coordination is a prerequisite for top performance. Athletes use a lot of muscles to enable them to carry out movements directly, quickly, powerfully and enduringly over long periods of time. They therefore need a well-developed nervous system to control these muscles.

Technique-oriented coordination conditioning

When players concentrate too much on the sport-specific techniques that follow the agility ladder, there is a danger that they will carry out the tasks in the ladder carelessly. The coach should correct errors immediately and instruct the players to concentrate on both areas (coordination drills/soccer techniques).

Running coordination

Modern soccer is characterized by the speed at which it is played. The players are under pressure to act quickly both when they have the ball and when they don't. They have to make sprints into space, sudden changes of direction, switch from attack to defense and vice versa, etc. The demands on a soccer player are so great that special and systematic conditioning of their running coordination, and especially their running technique and timing, is essential. Soccer-specific conditioning of running coordination is thus gaining in importance as an element of training programs of soccer players at all levels.

Special aspects of running coordination

The demands made on soccer players, in terms of running, differ from those on a track athlete. Jumps, changes of direction, runs with the ball and tackles before or after a sprint require continuous adjustment of stride length and frequency to the rapidly changing circumstances of the game. Variable, flexible and appropriate use of running techniques is essential during a game. With the agility ladder, players can practice the necessary forms of movement (running and jumping movements). The ladder is an indispensable part of modern soccer conditioning.

Fast footwork

Targeted condition of the running coordination of soccer players requires prioritization of the different elements of running coordination during the training sessions. Fast footwork, i.e. the rapid coordination of nerves and foot muscles, is one of the most important of these elements. Speed and high step frequencies are enormously important in modern soccer and are the main objective of working with the agility ladder. When a player takes short, fast steps, he is able to change direction at any moment. He can control his body and accelerate quickly in any given direction. He should be able to emerge from a short-stepping one-against-one situation and switch quickly to a long-striding sprint.

Footwork and shooting

Good footwork is the basis for good shooting technique. Only by continuously adjusting the distance between ball and foot can a player get into the best shooting position. This also applies to controlling a pass under pressure and jumping to head the ball. A player's ability to adjust his position relative to the ball is enormously important.

Word of thanks

I would like to thank all the players who helped with the photos, and coaches Ludger Blaswich, Achim Nohlen and Peter Hyballa, for their help and encouragement. In particular I would like to thank Marion Becker-Richter. Her support in the fields of digital processing and graphic layout made the numerous photos and drawings possible.

Drills without a ball

The practical part of this book starts with general coordination conditioning. There are three main aspects:
✓ Running
✓ Jumping
✓ Combinations of running and jumping.

Running forward

'One touch' means that the players make one step per field. The coach focuses on correct arm movement (opposite arm forward in time with the leg movement, with elbow angle approximately 90 degrees). 'Two touch' means that the players carry out two fast steps in one field. The swing of the arms should be adjusted to the faster movement of the legs. The players must run on the balls of their feet.

One touch   **Two touch**

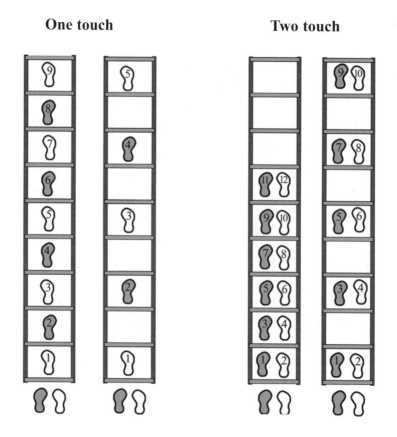

Combination: One and two touch

The players run along the first part of the agility ladder in one-touch mode. When they pass the two cones at the center, they switch to two-touch mode. This drill promotes body control and coordination for a fast change of rhythm. This applies especially to the change in the speed of the arm movement. The objective of this drill is to make the adjustment of the arm movement to the leg movement automatic.

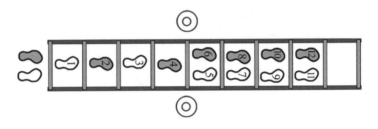

One foot out

The players run with one foot inside the agility coordinator and the second foot outside. The players must take care not to tread on the agility ladder. This additional task must not impair their running technique.

Dummy step (with tap)

The ability to suddenly stop and change direction is required in many sports. This can be practiced with the agility ladder. The players zigzag along the agility ladder in two-touch mode. They check the sideways movement with a tap step (without shifting their weight). Immediately after this tap touch to the ground, the players set off to the other side.

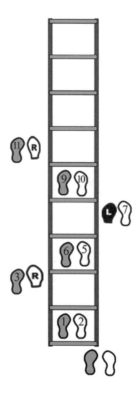

Hopping

Hopping along the agility ladder is difficult, and not just for young players. This is especially true when the players have to concentrate on what they are doing. The players often swing the arm on the same side as the hopping leg forward rather than the one on the opposite side.

Hopping along the agility ladder represents an increase in the level of difficulty, as a number of aspects have to be coordinated: arm and leg movements, and landing and take-off in the fields, without touching the agility ladder.

There are three variations:
✓ Simple hopping
✓ Jump-hopping (powerful swing of the arms; higher jump)
✓ Sideways hopping

Running movements - sideways

Sidesteps - Two touch

The players must avoid tensing up. They must swing their arms and achieve a fast tempo.

Start by standing at one end of the ladder (see diagram). Move the left foot into the first field of the agility ladder, leaving sufficient space for the right foot in the same field. Use the arms to support the fast running tempo.

Changes of direction

Perform two or three sidesteps along the ladder, then reverse direction and return to the first field. The change of direction can best be carried out with a tap step, just touching the foot briefly to the ground without shifting the weight onto it.

Sidesteps: 3 forward - 1 back

Sidesteps: 2 forward - 1 back

Cross-step, front

This drill is very good for the mobility of the hips. The upper body should be kept as still as possible. Start by standing at one end of the ladder (see diagram). Draw the right leg across the front of the left leg and place the right foot in the first field. Each step is into the next field.

In this example, the right leg crosses in front of the left leg.

Cross step, back
Draw the right leg across the back of the left leg.

Cross step, alternating
This is the most difficult version of the cross-step and requires a certain amount of practice and concentration so that the movements appear rhythmic and harmonious.

✓ Right leg across front of left
✓ Left foot in next field
✓ Right foot across back of left
✓ Left foot in next field
etc.

Backward and forward steps - sideways
Step from field to field with the lead foot (in this example, the left),
moving the trailing leg alternately forward and back.

The sequence is as follows:
✓ Start by placing the left foot in the first field
✓ Place the right foot forward
✓ Place the left foot in the next field
✓ Place the right foot backward
etc.

Backward and forward steps - leading with the right foot.

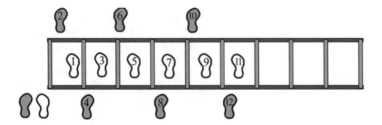

✓ Lead with the right foot
✓ Always place the right foot in the next field
✓ Move the left foot alternately forward and back

Running backward

Players often have to move backward quickly, taking short steps, without stumbling. In the agility ladder they are forced to concentrate and place their feet precisely in the fields. It is advisable to turn the head slightly to the side and look back over the shoulder.

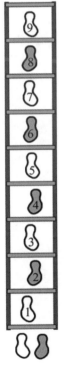 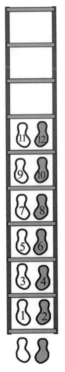

Diagram, left: One touch
The players run backward along the agility ladder (one step per field)

Diagram, right: Two touch
Both feet have to touch the ground in each field. The coach can support the running tempo by calling out one-two, one-two, etc.

Complex running movements and changes of direction

Combination: Forward - sideways
The directions can be combined at will.

- ✓ Forward - sideways
- ✓ Forward - backward
- ✓ Forward - sideways - backward

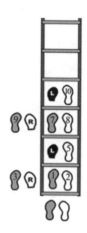

Without change of side:
2 forward - left -
2 forward - left

With change:
2 forward - left -
2 forward - right

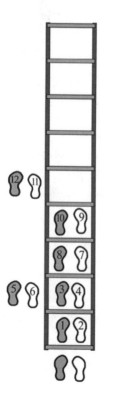

Combination: Forward - backward

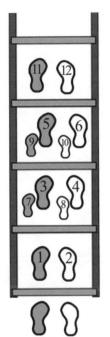

Two-touch run with change of direction:

✓ Left, right
✓ Left, right
✓ Left, right
✓ Left back, right back
✓ Left forward, right forward
etc.

One-touch run and change of direction with two-contact steps

✓ Three steps forward (1, 2, 3)
✓ Adjustment steps (into next field, 4, 5)
✓ Adjustment step backward (6, 7)
✓ Next three steps (8, 9, 10)

Jumps

The following jumps can be carried out in the agility ladder:

✓ Two-footed jumps forward
✓ Sideways jumps across the agility ladder
✓ Jumping jack (opening and closing the legs)
✓ One-footed jumps
✓ Sideways jumps along the agility ladder
✓ Backward jumps
✓ Jump and turn
✓ Combinations (direction - type of jump).

Two-footed jumps - forward

Diagram, left:
Jump into each field

Diagram, right:
Jump into each second field

Jumps over cones

The cones in every other field of the coordination ladder serve as orientation aids. In addition, they force the players to jump higher.

Jumps with changes of direction

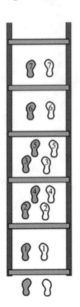

The direction of the jumps can be changed in a regular pattern. The diagram shows a pattern of 3 jumps forward and 1 back.

Variation: 2 forward - 1 back

Jumping jack

An important drill for improving arm and leg coordination is the jumping jack. With its numerous variants, it enables the coach to set lots of movement tasks. The first variant makes use of the forward jump.

Variation A   **Variation B**

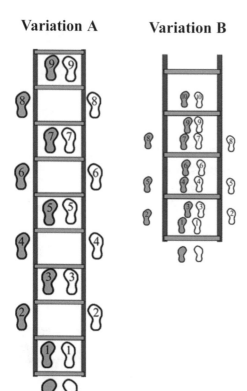

Variation A:
The player always jumps into a new field.

Variation B:
The jumping jack movement (open - close) is always carried out in one field before the player jumps forward to the next field.

Combination of jumping jack and jump forward

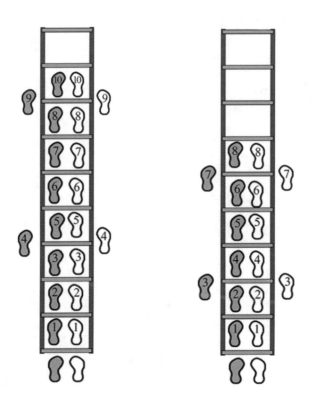

Jumping jack
over cones

Sideways jumps across the agility ladder

The player jumps from left to right, placing one foot inside the ladder and one foot outside as he lands. The feet should point forwards slightly diagonally.

This jump is very good for the balance and coordination of the leg movements.

Important:
The players should hold the upper body vertical and let the lower legs do the work.

One-footed jumps - forward

Take care:
These jumps put a lot of stress on the joints! The players should have strong leg muscles and must not hop for too long on one leg (alternate between right and left!).

Diagram A)
One-footed jumps, alternating after two jumps

Diagram B)
One-footed jumps, alternating after three jumps

The switch from one leg to the other can also be carried out after four jumps.

A)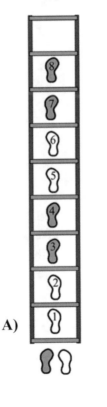

B)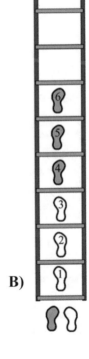

Variations on one-footed jumps

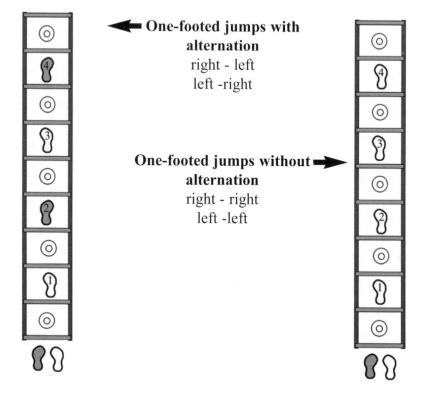

◄ One-footed jumps with alternation
right - left
left -right

**One-footed jumps without ►
alternation**
right - right
left -left

Combination of one-footed and two-footed jumps

A)	**B)**	**C)**
Hop - hop - two-footed	Hop - two-footed - hop - two footed	Alternating the take-off foot

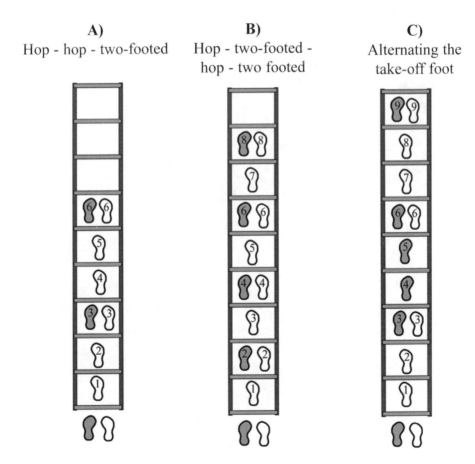

Sideways jumps along the agility ladder

Sideways jumps can be carried out in two ways:

a) Rungs between the feet (photo left)
b) Both feet in one field (diagram).

Sideways zigzag along the agility ladder (forward - backward)

The player carries out two-footed jumps forward and diagonally backward, thus moving along the agility ladder.

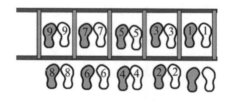

Sideways jumps across the agility ladder and over cones

The players start by standing side-on to the cones, which are placed in every second field. The players alternately jump sideways over the cones and hop diagonally forward into the next field (see diagram).

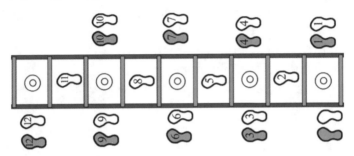

Jump and turn
The degree of difficulty increases when the players have to jump and turn. The players should keep their upper bodies as vertical as possible and twist them as little as possible.

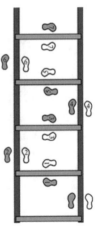

Jump and turn, legs apart

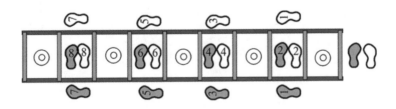

Combinations of running and jumping movements

Switching between one-footed and two-footed jumps is especially good for developing a sense of rhythm. It is important that the players start using both feet and master a variety of combinations. This is essential to the development of good coordination. After the final jump a change of feet can be introduced. This increases the level of difficulty.

Example: left - right - left - hop - right - left - right.

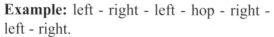

Diagram, left:
left - right - hop - left - right - hop

Variation: Change of feet

Diagram, right:
right - left - hop - hop

Variation:
right - left - right - left - hop -hop

Combinations of running movements and sideways jumps across the ladder

Diagram, left:
Sideways jumps across the ladder while moving forward

Diagram, right:
Sideways jumps across the ladder in one field (left/right).

Fast steps + jumping jack

This is an important coordination-oriented drill: the change from a running movement to the jumping jack.

Two variations are shown below.

Diagram A:
right - left - right- left - hop - open - close

Diagram B:
right - left - right- left - open - close

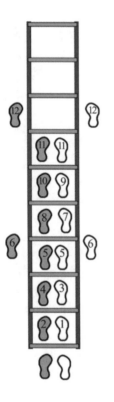

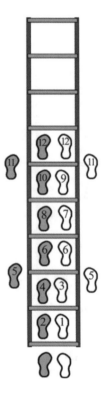

Diagram A   **Diagram B**

Complex running and jumping movements for advanced players

Left: Run - hop - jumping jack
Rhythm: Right - left - right - hop (4) - jumping jack (5, 6), etc.

Center: Run - hop forward and back
Rhythm: Left - right - left - hop forward (4) - hop back (5), etc.

Right: Run - hop - open
Rhythm: Right (1) - hop (2) - open (3) - right (4) - hop (5) - open (6), etc.

left   center   right

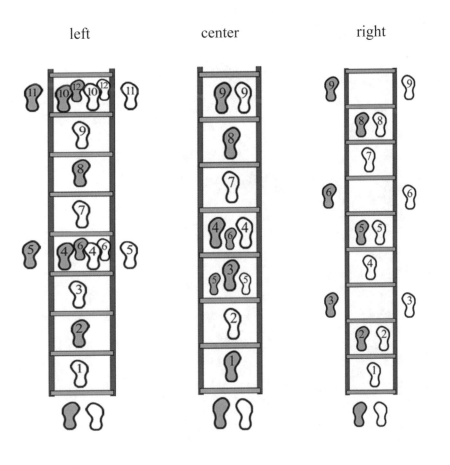

Arm and leg coordination

Keep arms in one position

Stretch arms upward

Stretch arms forward

Stretch arms to the side

Arms behind head

Arms crossed in front of chest

Move arms to parts of body

Move hand to thigh while skipping

Variation:
Inside of foot, instep.

Hold ball in specified position

Hold the ball in front of or behind the body

Variation:
Hold the ball in the air or with arms stretched forward

Move ball in specified ways

Up - down

Forward - back

Move ball to part of body

Move ball to thigh

Variation: Inside of foot, instep

Move ball in circle around body

Circle ball around body while running

Bounce ball (with one hand)

Foot and ball movements must be synchronized. If the foot movements are fast (two touch), the ball must be bounced quickly and low.

Bounce ball (with both hands)

Two touch run while simultaneously bouncing the ball with both hands

Jumping jack + bouncing the ball (no more than hip high)

Variation:
- Throw the ball in the air and catch it (no more than head high)
- Clap hands before catching the ball

Drills with a ball

The coach has a ball in his hands and throws it to the player carrying out a sequence of movements in the agility ladder. As the player moves forward toward the coach, the coach moves backward. In this drill the player heads the ball while carrying out jumps in the agility ladder.

Coordination-oriented technique conditioning

Technique conditioning with additional tasks improves coordination. The players have to focus on a second task as well as their soccer technique.

There should be a lot of variation in the movement tasks in
the agility ladder, so that the
players have to concentrate all
the time.

Volleys with inside of foot -
combined with dummy steps

Volleys with instep - combined
with running movements (two
touch forward)

Hip high volley on the turn
with left and right foot alternately - combined with sidesteps

Follow-up tasks after the agility ladder

The tasks in the agility ladder are now connected with soccer techniques. The follow-up tasks should not pose any technical problems, so that the whole sequence can flow smoothly.
Note: Coordination conditioning involves carrying out acquired, mastered movements while coping with added difficult factors.

Pass from the goal - sprint to the ball - pass back to the coach or shoot at goal

Pass from the side - pass to second player or shoot at goal

Continuous format:
Six to eight players practice with an agility ladder. One player stands with a ball a few yards away from the end of the agility ladder. He throws the ball to the second player and catches the ball when the second player heads it back. The players then swap positions and the player with the ball gives it to the other.

Combinations with other coaching aids

The coach has innumerable variation options when he combines the agility ladder with other coaching aids.

Combination with hurdles

Combination with hoops

Hurdles combined with agility ladder
The players carry out a task in the starting zone (hurdles) before they turn to the agility ladder, in which they carry out a second task.

Hoop course with agility ladder

Ladder at 90 degrees

When the coaching aids are laid out in different ways, the players must concentrate harder when they move from one aid to another. This is especially so when a change of task is also included. This coaching format could combine, for example, a slalom run and sidesteps.

Hoops - rods - agility ladder

The diagram shows hoops and rods positioned at 90 degrees to the agility ladder. This arrangement can be used in various ways.

Example:
Start with the hoop course - Task in the agility ladder - Task in the rod course

The tasks in the three sections should be continuously varied. Advanced players are capable of coordinating three different ball and leg movements.

Agility ladder and shooting

There are two ways of introducing the ball into play:
a) The player takes the ball himself, carries out a few tasks with it in the agility ladder, throws the ball a few yards away, runs to it and shoots at goal.
b) The player starts without a ball, receives a pass or a throw from the coach and shoots or heads the ball at goal.

The player throws the ball in the air at the end of the agility ladder and shoots at goal with a hip-high volley on the turn.

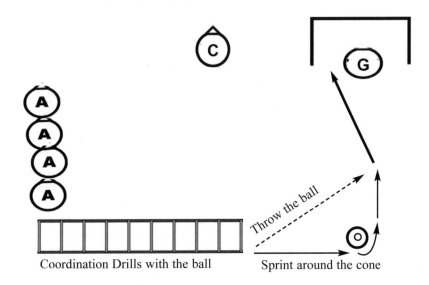

Coordination Drills with the ball   Sprint around the cone

The coach should vary the additional tasks in the agility ladder (see drills with a ball).

The coach tells the player how to shoot and which foot to use. The agility ladder can be set up at 90 or 180 degrees to the goal.

The coach or a second player passes the ball

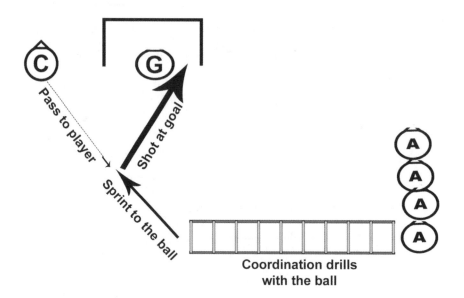

Coordination drills
with the ball

Complex drills

The agility ladder can be easily combined with other coaching aids. The coach therefore has innumerable options for devising complex drills. The players learn to adjust their movements continuously to new tasks.

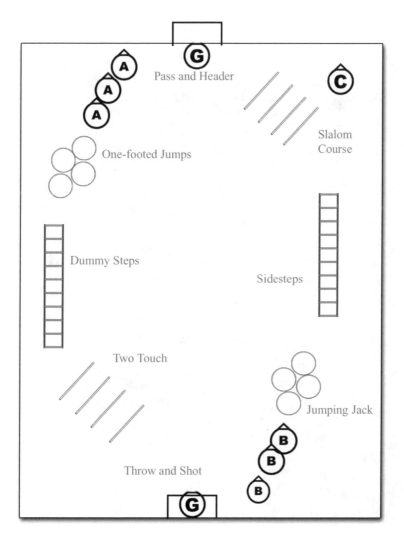

Two-player drills

The agility ladder can be used for two-player drills. This opens up new possibilities, as the players have to concentrate on a moving target and adjust their movements to those of the second player. In the following drill, the players move toward each other. At the center of the agility ladder, which is marked by two cones, the players carry out a task (high fives and run back, run past each other, turn, etc.).

Two-player drills with a ball

Two-player drills with a ball are very popular. One player carries out a coordination task, while the second player runs parallel to him. The tasks can vary widely:

The simplest drill is touching the ball. The player in the agility ladder moves the ball back and forth and the second player touches the ball. The ball can also be handed back and forth. It is important that the player in the agility ladder retains his running rhythm.

In the next phase the second player throws the ball to the player in the agility ladder. It is not easy to head the ball back while carrying out a coordination task at the same time.

When the ladder is arranged in a right angle, the coach can combine two different running movements (two-touch run forward and sidesteps) with tasks with a ball.

Goalkeeper conditioning with the agility ladder

Goalkeepers must be able to change direction quickly when making short fast foot movements (running movements, jumps), in order to gain and keep possession of the ball. A good sense of timing is essential to enable a goalkeeper to react to game situations with the necessary speed. The agility ladder conditions this sense of timing and can thus be used to prepare goalkeepers for typical game situations. The agility ladder can be set up at 45, 90 or 180 degrees to the goal, depending on the coaching objective. The ball can be on the ground or can be thrown by a second player or the coach. The agility ladder is an excellent coaching aid for goalkeeper-specific physical and coordination conditioning.

In this drill the goalkeepers have to run along the agility ladder with small fast sidesteps and then dive sideways onto a ball.

Depending on the distance of the ball from the agility ladder, the goalkeeper can touch the ball or grasp it with both hands.

Tasks involving sideways movements

The goalkeepers have the task of moving from one end of the agility ladder to the other sideways (sidesteps, jumps, backward and forward steps, etc.) and diving to the ball when the coach throws it at waist or head height.

In this drill the coach shoots along the ground. The goalkeeper must quickly switch from the sideways movement and dive to the ground to secure the ball.

Sideways reaction while in the agility ladder

The coach moves backward and throws the ball to the right or left of the goalkeeper. The goalkeeper has to perform a set sequence of steps before diving to the ball.

The goalkeeper must quickly convert the rhythm of his run into a dive to the ball.

Variations:
- Sidesteps
- Sideways jumps across the agility ladder
- Two-footed jumps
- One-footed jumps

Coordination drills with additional tasks

The goalkeepers traverse the agility ladder and then carry out tasks involving goalkeeping techniques (catching a high ball, securing a ball, diving to stop a shot). Several goalkeepers can take part in this continuous drill.

Variation:
The coach shoots along the ground (from the front or side) and the goalkeepers dive to secure the ball.

Peter Schreiner (b. 1953):

✓ Head of the Institut für Jugendfussball
  (Institute for Youth Soccer)
  (www.ifj96.de)
✓ Co-founder of the Deutsche Fussball-
  Akademie (German Soccer Academy)
  (www.dfa-web.de)
✓ Author of the book
  "Coordination, Agility and Speed
  Training for Soccer" and the video
  "Coordination and Agility Training
  with a Soccer Ball"
✓ Lecturer at national and international soccer education events
✓ Author of numerous articles in soccer journals

About this book:

More and more coaches are discovering the agility ladder for conditioning speed, agility and coordination. Peter Schreiner has collected
numerous drills in this book, which will help coaches to organize varied coaching sessions on these themes. Clear diagrams and photos
ensure that the drills and information are presented attractively and
comprehensibly.

Topics:

✓ Drills without a ball (running conditioning, arm and leg coordina-
  tion)
✓ Coordination conditioning with a ball
✓ Two-player drills
✓ Use of the agility ladder for goalkeeper conditioning

Photo credits:
The game scene on page 5 is from Eventyret Drillos, p. 127, Schibsted-
Verlag.

More Titles from Peter Schreiner available from Reedswain Publishing:

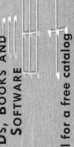
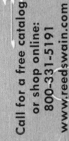
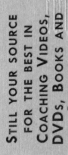